CHANGE

change the way you think about change

ASTD Press is an internationally renowned source of insightful and practical information on workplace learning and performance topics, including training basics, evaluation and return-on-investment, instructional systems development, e-learning, leadership, and career development.

Ordering Information: Books published by ASTD Press can be purchased by visiting ASTD's website at store.astd.org or by calling 800.628.2783 or 703.683.8100.

Library of Congress Control Number: 2010938873

ISBN-10: 1-56286-748-2
ISBN-13: 978-1-56286-748-5

ASTD Press Editorial Staff:

Director: Adam Chesler
Manager, ASTD Press: Jacqueline Edlund-Braun
Project Manager, Content Acquisition: Justin Brusino
Senior Associate Editor: Tora Estep
Associate Editor: Victoria DeVaux
Editorial Assistant: Stephanie Castellano
Copyeditor: Victoria DeVaux

Proofreader: Victoria DeVaux
Graphic Design: Yvette Tam
Production: Steve Fife
Interior Illustration: Ramiro Alonso
Cover Design: Ana Ilieva Foreman
Printed by: Versa Press, Inc., East Peoria, Illinois;
www.versapress.com

the
CHANGE
BOOK  change the way you think about change

Tricia Emerson
Mary Stewart

1640 King Street Box 1443
Alexandria, VA 22313-1443 USA

t: 800.628.2783 703.683.8100
f: 703.683.8103 www.astd.org

CONTENTS

Preface   **vi**

Foreword   **viii**

Acknowledgements   **x**

SECTION 1: Framing   **1**

What Is Change Management?   2

Assume the Position   7

Vision: It's Got To Be Real   10

Frame the "Why?"   15

The Change Recipe   17

Scaling the Change   18

Do I Need a Message?   23

SECTION 2: Leadership and Teams   **34**

And Now, a Word From Our Sponsor   36

An Army of One   40

Are the Right People on the Team?   45

Don't Forget the Carrot   48

SECTION 3: Design   **54**

Structure Enables Change   56

Align Your Design   58

Four Truths of Organization Design   63

SECTION 4: Resistance   **68**

The Hecklers   70

A State of Confusion   78

People Prefer the Predictable   85

We're Hardwired to Resist Change   88

Change Your Mind   92

Section 5: Culture   **96**

It's the Culture, Stupid!   98

Subculture Savvy   108

Section 6: Branding   **116**

Brand With Caution   118

Symbols Matter   124

Combating Existing Symbols   130

Section 7: Communication   **134**

Change Communication 101   137

The Big Shift   143

Not Communicating Is Communicating   147

I Already Told Them!   151

Be Willing to Say the Hard Things   157

Communication Gotchas   161

Section 8: Momentum   **164**

The Tipping Point   167

Don't Be Afraid to Engage the Masses   172

The Psychology of Signing On   174

Emotion: It's All In the Story   179

Map It   186

Stakeholders Get Weary   190

Section 9: Measurement   **194**

If a "change" happens in the woods…   197

PACE Yourself!   204

You are a **CHANGE MANAGEMENT** professional. You deal with organizational changes, big and small, every day. But change is hard, and sometimes even the best of us get stuck.

We wrote this book for people like ourselves—experienced, time-challenged professionals looking for ways to be more effective in managing change. The insights in this book are meant to help when you feel stalled. They are about the gotchas: the hard-won knowledge that comes from skinned knees and bumped heads. They might jump-start your creativity, give you a fresh idea, remind you of something that worked in the past, or simply change your perspective.

In addition to managing change, from time to time you must articulate the need for change management. This book gives you simple ideas and concepts that illustrate these needs and illuminate change methods for you, your clients, your teams, and your company leadership.

Change is simple. Our chapters are written to be short and easy to digest. Each contains just one "nugget of wisdom" from years of change consulting experience.

Change is flexible. Open to any chapter! No need to start at the beginning. Read the table of contents and pick something that interests you. Each chapter is self-contained, so read one or read them all, in any order you like.

Change is helpful. Periodically, a chapter will give you suggestions:

 This icon indicates a suggestion for other chapters you might want to read related to the current topic.

 Want to learn more about the topic? This icon references books, articles, and websites that will help you "go deep."

FOREWORD

Vibrant companies and organizations rejuvenate themselves. They change. Products, services, customers, employees, systems…they are all impermanent. Some have argued that companies need to follow the human body model. We're told the body replaces its cells every seven years. So if change is cyclical, why not do it well?

Change is stressful to both the individual and the organization, and people and organizations don't perform well under constant stress. That's what's unique about this book. It focuses on human performance. It focuses on the stressors you don't think about. It recommends how to renew and sustain performance during change, and how to provide meaning during chaotic times. Individual and organizational performance is multidimensional. That's what makes it complicated to manage. That's why you need help.

This book covers the essence of change in a fun way. There's a lot packed into these small pages, and the axioms ring true. Change is hard to do, but this easy read will reinforce the old, show you the new, and warn you of the pitfalls.

But with all this change, don't forget that some things stay the same: your company values for one, the higher principles from which your people and your organization operate for another. These remain constant; however, those values and principles need to be reinforced, reexamined, and recommitted to during stressful times of change. They will anchor you. That's why these human performance change professionals emphasize company culture.

These authors have done change over and over again. They get it. They have mastered it. And now you can too.

Carla J. Paonessa
Retired Global Managing Partner for Change
Accenture

ACKNOWLEDGEMENTS

One winter, our team of twenty shared some downtime sitting around a table and chatting about our client experiences. We realized that this lull in our workload was a wonderful opportunity to capture the best of what this group, some of the finest in the field, knew about change.

The group took on the task to "riff" on their expertise. "Don't write the basics," Trish said. "Write for people like yourselves: short on time, short on attention, but deep in expertise." And then Mary made sense of the output.

This book is the result of this labor. We worked on it monthly during company meetings for two years, and periodically in between. And while the content and form evolved during this time, the heart of it would not exist except for the efforts of the following contributors:

Farrow Adamson   **Rebecca Spiros**

Vicky Cavanaugh   **Mark Webster**

Darby Davenport   **Yvette Tam,** *Designer*

Hastie Karger   **Ramiro Alonso,** *Illustrator*

Kim Lewis   **Carol Irvine,** *Photographer*

Bettina Rousos   **Genevieve Shiffrar,** *Photographer*

Thanks to these people, and the entire Emerson Human Capital team, for their contribution, faith, and diligence, particularly when they were also juggling client obligations. Working with them remains one of our greatest joys!

Trish Emerson and Mary Stewart

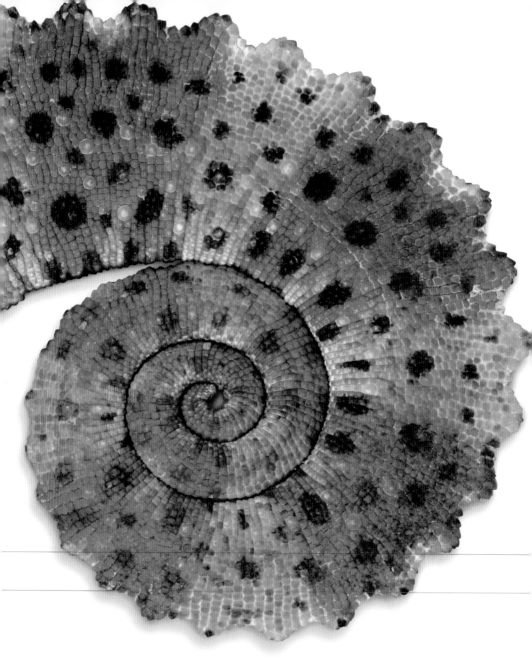

SECTION 1
Framing

What Is Change Management?

The "change" is an attempt to capture a benefit opportunity

The event initiating that change can be the introduction of a new strategy, new technology, new organization, or a new skill. And that event presents an opportunity to be successful at best, maintain status quo if we're lucky, or fail at worst.

The "management" targets human performance

Miss one element and the whole performance system breaks down.

STRATEGY: What is the overall purpose and direction for this initiative, and how will the change be managed?

INTERNALIZATION: What behavioral changes do we expect?

FOCUS: Have we appropriately directed people's attention to the change?

SUSTAINABILITY: What infrastructure ensures the change will continue?

We have to address all four elements at the individual and organizational level.

CHANGE MANAGEMENT

Helping organizations capture a benefit opportunity by influencing human performance.

Assume
the Position

Three ways to position change

THE BRIDGE: Make desired outcome the default

Sign people up. Make them opt out. Shut down the old system. Tell people the "givens" and offer choices within that framework.

THE COBRA: Compare the change to something scarier

Example | You were thinking about buying a ticket to Bermuda. It's $1,200 a ticket—no way! Suddenly you get an IM that a competitor is offering tickets for $2,000. You buy the $1,200 ticket and feel good about it.

Change-related Example | Our competitors close the books in four days. Our new process allows us to do it in two. It's all about perspective.

THE DOWNWARD DOG: Frame the change in negative terms

Negative messaging creates more dramatic movement.

IF YOU POSITION CHOICES AS:

Gains	|	people will take the lowest risk option.
Losses	|	people will take the highest risk option.

Nope	|	We are reorganizing to be operationally excellent!
Yep	|	We must reorganize or you will lose your job.

"HAPPY TALK" IS COMFORTABLE, BUT SCIENCE SHOWS THAT FEAR OF LOSS CREATES MOVEMENT. WANT IMPACT? FRAME THE URGENCY.

---

reference	This is based on Kahneman and Tvesky's prospect theory.

Vision: It's Got To Be Real

THIS MAN NEEDS A VISION.

Everyone knows you gotta have a vision. It establishes a shared understanding of the future state. But to gain genuine commitment, you've got to take that lofty vision and make it real.

You know you want to get to the moon, but how do you get there?

1. What are we going to do to achieve the vision? Think about tactics.

2. Why are we doing this? It needs to be desirable.

3. Paint the picture. What does it look like? What will there be more of? What will there be less of? Start thinking about what people will do differently on the first day after the change. Make it personal.

4. How will we know when we're there? What are our indicators of progress?

 Your Vision Needs a Good "Why." : pg 14

"Vision without a task is only a dream.
 A task without a vision is but drudgery.
 But vision with a task is a dream fulfilled."

– ANONYMOUS

Frame the "Why?"

Most projects fail to frame the need for change in a meaningful way. If they do justify the need, it's typically crafted for executive boardrooms, not for the broader organization.

To get support, there must be a shared understanding of the case for change. We must paint the picture – build a sense of urgency.

Start by answering these questions:

- ♦ What do we stand to gain?
- ♦ If we don't do it, what are the consequences?
- ♦ Which are short-term consequences?
- ♦ Which are long-term consequences?
- ♦ How can we amplify the urgency for change?

Consider your key constituents and frame the need for change in a way that speaks to each of them. Without meaningful framing, the project will struggle to gain traction. It's that simple.

Once You've Got It, Brand It : pg 118

The Change Recipe

JUMP-START YOUR CHALLENGING AND JUICY
CHANGE EFFORTS...WITH THE RIGHT INGREDIENTS

prep time 6 months

ingredients

Fresh dissatisfaction

1 cup vision (contains optimism)

Sprig of business knowledge

Dollop of expertise

1 cup project oversight

2 packs communication

Splash of shared values

1 Sponsor (at least 1 credible)

1 dozen stakeholders

Dash of beliefs

Zest of inspiration

Bundle of desired behaviors

Recognition (to taste)

preparation

1. Pre-heat dissatisfaction and bring to a boil. Keep warm.
2. Combine at least one sponsor and vision together; mix until smooth.
3. Slowly fold in strategy and add a pack of communication.
4. Pair business knowledge and expertise with project oversight.
5. Add another pack of communication.
6. Whisk together beliefs and shared values, drizzled with inspiration to heat up end-users.
7. Transfer desired behaviors to end-users.
8. Season with recognition.

yields Digestible Change Efforts

Scaling
the Change

Pick an organism

THE BEE is a *transactional change.*
It's a change in a business capability. It's a change in the way people perform a task. You need people to change behaviors and attitudes. There's no significant resistance based on culture–you're not swimming against the tide. You need relatively minor change management.

THE BLOSSOM is an *operational change.*
It's a change in the way you operate the business. You need people to change the way they do their jobs and the way they think about their jobs. People must begin performing and communicating in new ways. You need major change management.

THE BUTTERFLY is a *transformational change.*
Sometimes called a paradigm shift. It's an irreversible shift in the status quo. It's radical, multidimensional and multilevel. It's a change in who you are as a business. It's a change in how people think about themselves and their jobs. You are changing people's reality. You need people to change their perceptions, beliefs, and to identify with their jobs in a different way. You need fundamental change management.

THE LEVEL OF CHANGE
TRANSACTIONAL, OPERATIONAL, OR TRANSFORMATIONAL DETERMINES
THE DEPTH AND SCALE OF THE CHANGE MANAGEMENT EFFORT. INVEST
IN RESOURCES APPROPRIATELY. A BIG CHANGE MEANS BIG THINKERS,
BIG SOLUTIONS, AND SIGNIFICANT ENERGY.

LEVEL OF CHANGE	EXAMPLES	LEVEL OF CHANGE MGMT	EXAMPLES
TRANSACTIONAL	Your company is introducing a new product to its line.	Minor	One key sponsor. Communication to company. Targeted training to sales and marketing.
OPERATIONAL	Your organization is implementing ERP (Enterprise Resource Planning) across business units.	Major	Sponsors from all business units. Dedicated change-agent team. Layered sponsorship and communication plans. Intensive end-user training. Support and transition.
TRANSFORMATIONAL	Your company has been acquired by an enterprise with a completely different culture and identity, and they will change your whole business model.	Fundamental	All-hands sponsorship effort. Culture mapping and transition. Re-branding and marketing effort. Organization and job redesign. Massive buy-in and communication plan, including external audiences. Training for all new and affected employees. Long-term transition plan.

Do I Need a Message?

I don't know.
You tell me.

If you asked three sponsors what the change was about, would they describe it consistently?

Can you distill your strategy into three or four main points?

Do you know who you are trying to reach?

Are you sharing your strategy or what your target audience really needs to hear?

Are you using the right facts? Reinforcing the right analogies?

Are you culturally in tune?

Ok.
Then what is a message?

A well-crafted message is the fundamental building block of all successful communication.

It is short, simple and easy to remember.

It is the "30-second elevator speech." A message is the 30,000-foot view, the distillation of everything into a simple, compelling argument.

It is easy to visualize. It is three or four major points that you can communicate graphically by a triangle or box shape. This will help the messenger easily remember the major points that score with their target audience. (This comes from politics!)

Each major point is buttressed by a set of key words, quotes, or facts.

I STILL DON'T GET IT.

Think of messages like pieces of meat used to distract the dog guarding the jewels.

They are the best arguments you have. They grab attention, answer a burning problem, refute perceived weaknesses, highlight strengths.

They get you to the jewels: the stakeholder's support, their vote, their business, their financial help, or their good will.

I'm ready. What do I do?

Gather key players.

Discuss your project's strategy and goals.

Distill those goals into key words.

Review your company culture.

Understand your target audience.

Take an honest assessment of the good, bad and ugly your project may create.

List the results of your discussion—does it tell a story? Is it only your strategy? Only good news?

Use a message development template to focus your project goals, strengths, and challenges.

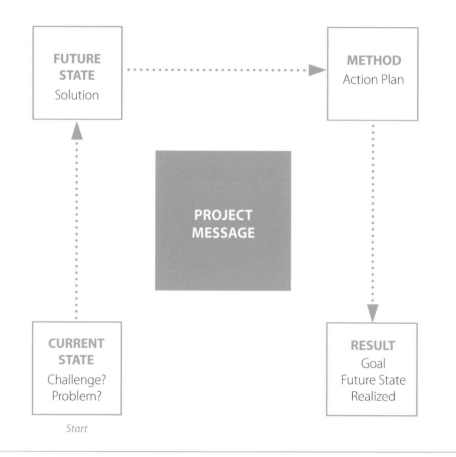

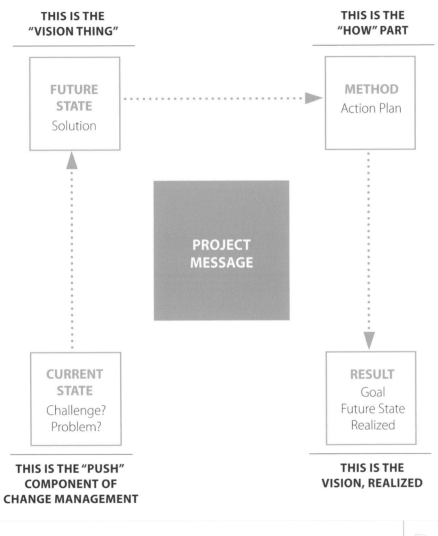

THIS IS THE "VISION THING"

FUTURE STATE
Solution

THIS IS THE "HOW" PART

METHOD
Action Plan

PROJECT MESSAGE

CURRENT STATE
Challenge?
Problem?

RESULT
Goal
Future State
Realized

THIS IS THE "PUSH" COMPONENT OF CHANGE MANAGEMENT

THIS IS THE VISION, REALIZED

REVOLUTION

By **transforming** our brand

By **meeting** changing guests needs

By **redefining food and beverage**, public spaces, technology, and other choices

Key words: *transformation, solution, modernization, overhaul*

Example: *smart, energizing, choices*

CONNECTION

By **sharing** the implementation and **owning** this solution together

By **investing** in tools

By **harnessing** your input in the pilot phase

Key words: *dialogue, turn-key hotels, end to end process, implementation check list*

Facts: *trainers there eight days before and three days after; series of five lunch and learns*

"REFRESHING" BUSINESS
Hotel Chain
Example

THREAT

From **changing** guests needs

From **growing** competitive landscape

From **evolving** market conditions

CONNECTION

To **lead** your teams

To **advance** your career

To **serve** our guests

We have a message!
How do we know it's good?

Check it. A good message is not:

- a treatise on everything an organization/project does
- the problem it seeks to solve
- everything to everyone
- merely a brand or slogan
- only positive.

So roll it out and then pay attention.

Your message is no good if you're:

- often pulled off-message
- constantly reacting to critics
- forced to address issues unrelated to your core message.

Beware of Symbols : pg 124
Start With Change Communication : pg 137

Leadership and Teams

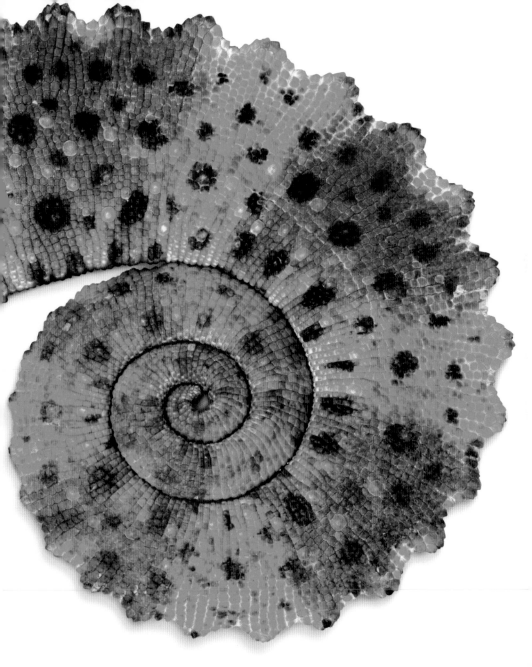

"And Now,
a Word From
Our Sponsor…"

A sponsor is critical to any change initiative. A sponsor points out the target on the horizon. A sponsor clears the way, provides the fuel, and keeps everyone on-course. A sponsor is the heart of the change.

Ready to Start Talking? Three Ways to Position Change : pg 7

WHAT WORDS DO YOU HEAR FROM *YOUR* SPONSOR?

"I know where we need to go."
A good sponsor must have the skill to lay out and communicate a compelling vision for the future.

"I'm excited."
A good sponsor is there because she wants to be. A sponser has a vested, personal interest in seeing the change succeed.

"I'm all in."
A good sponsor has the strength and the political capital to be held accountable for the project's results.

"I'll make it happen."
A good sponsor has the power to make the necessary decisions and allocate resources.

"Leave them to me."
A good sponsor has the relationships and influence to get other leaders to commit resources and time.

"You know I wouldn't steer you wrong."
A good sponsor has the respect of employees.

GOT SPONSORSHIP?

Some organizations create sponsorship at a very high level and much too late. If the project succeeds, the sponsor is a hero. The sponsor of a failed project is a goat.

Make sure your sponsor is a hero by setting up metrics. Agree on metrics in each category before the project begins—number of resources, numbers of communications or events, acceptable training attendance, number of employees "certified," and measurable changes in satisfaction or productivity. Measure as you go, and adjust the numbers if they aren't realistic.

SPONSORSHIP DIAGNOSIS

RESOURCES. Did the sponsor secure adequate funding for the project? Were the right resources made available, with the right skills, in the right numbers?

ORGANIZATION ALIGNMENT. Is the sponsor clearing the way for project success? Are there competing or contradictory initiatives going on? Are there any messages from other executives that undermine this effort?

KICKOFFS, TRAINING, AND OTHER EVENTS. Are people showing up? Are they showing up prepared? Are departments or individuals pushing back on requests from the project team or the sponsor? Or are they showing active support for the initiative?

COMMUNICATION. What communication? Is anything happening? How many times? How many channels? How effective are they? Survey employees: Did the sponsor communicate with them? What do they remember? What can they articulate?

2 TIPS

Look at sponsorship early and often.

Focus on what's observable.

An Army of One

Doomed to defeat

A sponsor without a team is like an army of one. A leader owns the vision, but a leader alone cannot implement that vision. The leader needs a band of operatives working at all levels of the organization: loyal and impassioned captains, lieutenants, and troops.

Leadership is necessary…but not sufficient.

 Does Your Project Have Good Sponsorship? : pg 36

CREATE AN ARMY FOR CHANGE

SPONSORS ARE THE GENERALS

- Own the mission
- Set direction and course
- Clear obstacles
- Marshall resources
- Lead the team toward its highest objective

PROJECT LEADS ARE THE CAPTAINS

- Have deep knowledge of how the army works and how to get the most out of it
- Develop battle plans
- Work the plans day-to-day
- Identify issues and risks
- Lead the team toward each interim objective

INFLUENCERS ARE THE LIEUTENANTS

- Have key relationships
- Influence and spur teams to action
- Spread the word about plans and tactics
- Celebrate reaching each objective

CHANGE AGENTS ARE THE TROOPS

- Communicate what we're fighting for
- Use their unique skills on the ground
- Have the pride of an elite force

UNDERSTAND YOUR OBJECTIVE

The goal of your force is not just to implement your change strategy.

Your goal is winning the hearts and minds of your workforce.

That means understanding your primary stakeholders. These are the end-users that will have to change their behavior. What are they feeling? How should you talk to them? What level of support works best?

Ask your change agents.

They are on the ground. They are newly equipped with change training.

Ask your influencers.

They have street cred. They can deliver the tough messages when needed.

Are the Right People on the Team?

Kick-Off

What criteria should you use to choose your team?

BAD CRITERIA

Role. Choosing people based on title or level does not ensure you have the most influential people. Don't mistake title for impact.

Politics. Placing people on a team to win internal points is a wonderful way to lose points. You want credibility and effectiveness.

Availability. Accepting people whose qualifications include "expendable" will mire your team. You need vital, agile, results-focused players. And guess what? So does everyone else.

GOOD CRITERIA

Knowledge, Skill, and Talent. Choose people who know the business. You will know you have the right person if the business doesn't want to give them up. These people are vital to successful deployment.

Influence. You need people who have impact. Choose people who are credible, known for their good work, and natural leaders.

Support. Your team members must support the change. Their attitude affects the quality of their work, team effectiveness, and their ability to be ambassadors for the change.

Constructing a team is a negotiation. Arming yourself with clear criteria for each role will help the organization assemble the team it needs to succeed.

Time Out

What if you've chosen poorly? Or you had to make some compromises on teammates? The wrong players make a bad team, and poor team dynamic is a killer. It affects efficiency, perception of the change, and quality of the work.

Back to the beginning: When you are staffing your team, talk about the risks of a poor team member. Set up a plan for mitigating these risks, including assessment, development, and replacement.

When the issues arise: Put your plan into action. Discussions about team member performance are tough, but essential to success.

Don't Forget
the Carrot

How do you keep a team engaged and moving on a change initiative? There isn't one right answer. But we know that people repeat a behavior that's successful.

What's the carrot? There are many choices.

FOR THE GROUP

A change project can feel like a roller coaster. Good teams have their eye on the ultimate goal, but sometimes that's not enough to get them past those dips and up the next hill. Select valuable and interesting rewards and deliver them when your team needs a boost.

GROUP CARROTS:

- non-work-related team event
- a write-up and photo of the team in a company publication
- something funny or something with personal meaning to the team.

A WORD OF CAUTION:

DON'T CELEBRATE TOO BIG, TOO EARLY. REWARDING THE TEAM PREMATURELY SENDS A MIXED MESSAGE ABOUT REWARD FOR RESULTS. CELEBRATE MAJOR MILE-STONES, COMPLETION OF TOUGH ASSIGNMENTS, PROJECT COMPLETION, AND MEETING ULTIMATE PROJECT GOALS.

FOR THE INDIVIDUAL

It's highly motivating to hear what you have done well. Praise is best when it's **specific** and delivered close to performance.

PERSONAL CARROTS:

- a verbal pat on the back, in an email, sent to the team
- an acknowledgement on the project intranet home page
- recognition during a team meeting
- any of the group carrots, but given to one person for outstanding performance
- a hand-written note.

Personal carrots need to be personal. Insincere or blanket praise can feel wrong, and you'll get the opposite of your intended result. Make it specific, real, and tie it to the team's goals. It takes observation, note-taking, and focus to do it right!

Bad | "You're a really hard worker."
Bad | "Great job."
Good | "Sally, when you created that job aid, mapping old codes to new ones, you saved users hours of effort. That helped us meet our goal to reduce costs and free people from work that doesn't add value. Great job!"

TIPS

- Plan the rewards as carefully as you would communication. Otherwise, you might forget them in the heat of battle.

- Small and easy works! Verbal recognition, a secretly prompted call from a sponsor, or acknowledgement in a meeting can have a huge impact.

- Borrow from gaming theory. Simple tracking and scoring can be rewarding. Publicly posting achievement of results makes a huge difference. And unrelated rewards (like robots marching down the screen when you win an online game) can be silly, but satisfying.

- Surprise is very important in rewards. We know from behaviorists that intermittent reinforcement given at varying intervals is more effective than rewards given on a predictable schedule. That's one reason gambling is so addictive.

THE FAN CLUB

There was a project manager who was a kick to work with and an extra-ordinary work planner. His peers talked about what a great guy he was and all considered themselves members of the "Paul Lambert Fan Club." Like every good fan club, this one had t-shirts made with Paul's picture on the front. On the appointed day, everyone wore them to the office.

THE RESULT

Paul got over his initial embarrassment and secretly liked the recognition. And the fan club was pleased with itself for being so clever in recognizing their comrade. Good feelings all around.

True Story

SECTION 3
Design

Structure
Enables Change

Want to institutionalize change? Make it sustainable? Then take a look at the organization's structure.

Successful change is changed behavior: the behavior that drives results. And internal structures can either **enable** or **block** those behaviors.

Whenever we embark on a change, we should examine the organization's structure to make sure it **facilitates** the behaviors we ultimately want.

It's likely our change requires a bit of organization design.

Align Your Design

Two scenarios cause the most trouble

GROWING PAINS

The company began when two entrepreneurs met in a smoky bar. Cocktail napkin in hand, they drew an org chart. It had accounting. It had finance. It had sales. It had the seeds of bloat that scaled as they added headcount to functional silos.

While romantic, this design isn't about how people work together to deliver what the customer values. It's about job functions.

The right design has a laser-like focus on the work processes that deliver value. We define jobs after we define the processes, in support of the processes. Functional silos are irrelevant.

A CALL TO ARMS

A new executive has joined the company. She has been given a charge: redesign this function! It's not effective – change it and deliver results.

She develops a new organization chart and changes teams and account-abilities. But the new function is still underperforming.

Why? Changing the org chart didn't address the toxic culture. Defining new functions or shifting boxes on an organization chart doesn't deliver results. In fact, these days employees have become more cynical, assuming a reorg is "the new executive making a mark." Edgar H. Shein, MIT professor, directly linked behavior to organization culture.

For a team: Behavior + Success = Repetition

Frequent Repetition = Culture

Our conclusion: Design an organization that facilitates successful behavior!

Four Truths
of Organization
Design

The Four Truths

[**1**] The organization's core competency distinguishes how it delivers customer value. Know what it is and design with that in mind.

[**2**] An organization structure exists to facilitate the work.

[**3**] Any work that does not deliver customer value should go away.

[**4**] Stakeholders are key to a good design. They create shared value and momentum for the change.

HERE'S HOW TO PUT THE TRUTHS INTO ACTION

MEETING 1: Make Me Smart

◆ Ask your customers, "What do you value from this organization?"

◆ Identify what success looks like.

◆ Call out the givens.

◆ Explore the latest thinking in designing these types of organizations.

◆ Identify your core competency (why your customers choose you).

◆ Determine who needs to buy into the final structure.

MEETING 2: Identify the Work

◆ Map out the major work that delivers customer value.

◆ Separate projects from ongoing work.

◆ Identify work that might be grouped together.

MEETING 3: Create Potential Organization Charts

♦ Agree on three types of organization qualities (e.g., flattest, cheapest, best supports company values).

♦ Brainstorm the structure that delivers the work based on the first quality.

♦ Include pros and cons.

♦ Choose the best of the set.

♦ Repeat with the second and third qualities.

♦ Brainstorm a structure that incorporates the best of the set from the three sessions.

♦ Create a final structure with pros and cons.

♦ **HOMEWORK:** Socialize with those who must buy in, and collect their feedback.

MEETING 4: Refine the Chart

♦ Report the feedback.

♦ Refine the design.

♦ Describe what this moves you "From - To": the vision driving the chart, the difference between the current and the future structure.

♦ Present to sponsors for feedback and sign-off.

CREATE JOB ROLE DESCRIPTIONS (TITLE, OBJECTIVES, KEY RESPONSIBILITIES, MEASURES) FOR HUMAN RESOURCES TO ESTIMATE WORK VOLUME (FREQUENCY, TIME) TO DETERMINE HEADCOUNT.

SECTION 4
Resistance

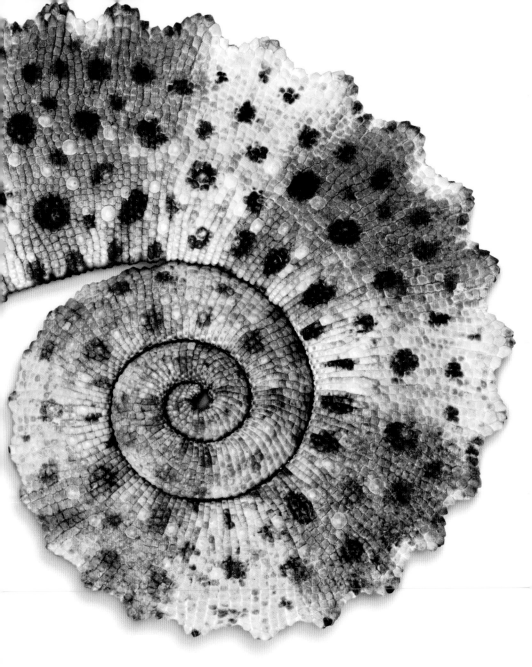

The Hecklers

Your change initiative is underway. But what's that? Do you hear the faint sound of booing? Is someone heckling you from the balcony? Any rotten tomatoes thrown your way?

That's to be expected. People resist change. It's natural. Resistance maintains order and the status quo.

Your hecklers might be:

- Saying negative things or showing negative emotions towards the change

- Predicting the change will fail

- Acting like the change has nothing to do with them or their team

- Refusing to provide resources or information

- Avoiding or not prioritizing project meetings, events, or training

- Missing important deadlines or working with no sense of urgency

- Refusing to try the new way or reverting to old ways.

How do you confront them?

You don't.

FIGURE OUT WHO HAS THE ABILITY TO
INFLUENCE THE SUCCESS OF THE PROJECT

Are some of them hecklers? Accept that you might not change them into fully supportive agents of this change.

Are some of them mildly resistant or mildly supportive? That's your sweet spot.

THE SWEET SPOT: AN EXAMPLE

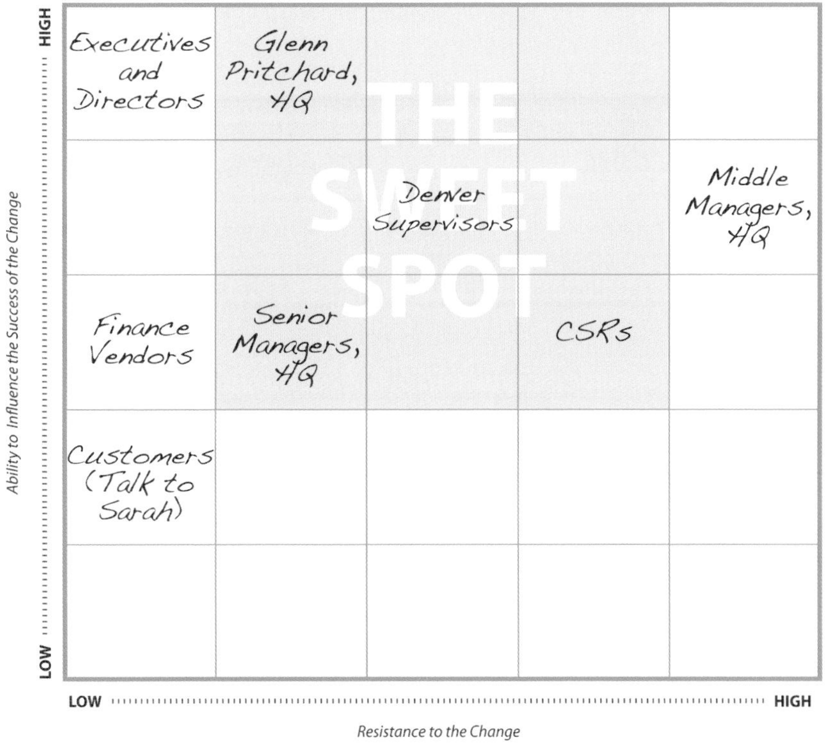
HIGH
LOW
Ability to Influence the Success of the Change
Executives and Directors
Glenn Pritchard, HQ
THE SWEET SPOT
Denver Supervisors
Middle Managers, HQ
Finance Vendors
Senior Managers, HQ
CSRs
Customers (Talk to Sarah)
LOW
HIGH
Resistance to the Change

NOW IT'S YOUR TURN—USE THESE TEMPLATES TO DISCOVER YOUR OWN SWEET SPOT

Roles   Locations

THE SWEET SPOT

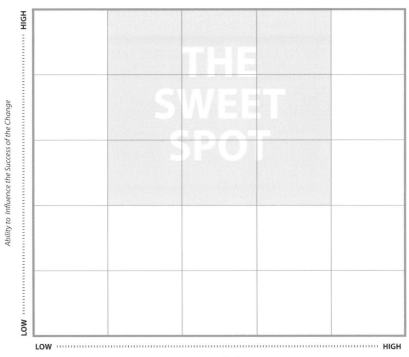

Ability to Influence the Success of the Change

HIGH

LOW

LOW .... HIGH

Resistance to the Change

THE SWEET SPOT

WHAT SHOULD YOU DO WITH THOSE IN YOUR SWEET SPOT?

Communication and **involvement** are your tools. For each group, ask:

What does this stakeholder group need to hear to make this change a priority? What do they care about? How does the change address that? What are the benefit opportunities for this group? What are the consequences of non-compliance?

How can we involve this stakeholder group so it begins to own the change? What communication or involvement opportunities exist in their world? On the project? What kinds of people are in this stakeholder group? What kinds of messages appeal to them? Who influences them? What are they good at? What do they like to do? What have they responded to in the past?

SO WE IGNORE THE HECKLERS?

No. We continue standing behind them through the change management plan: communicating, engaging, training, and supporting them. As other stakeholder groups become better change agents, your hecklers won't be so loud.

ONE CAVEAT:

MAKE IT CLEAR THAT CONSENSUS IS NOT THE GOAL. DISAGREEMENT CAN BE HEALTHY AND MAKE A BETTER END PRODUCT. INTERESTINGLY, MOST GROUPS SELF-REGULATE AND THROUGH FACILITATED DISCUSSION, REACH CONSENSUS NATURALLY.

A State
of Confusion

Every four years, on the first Tuesday in November, we elect a new president.

Every four years, on January 20, the new president takes office.

Question from actual nine-year-old: "What's up with that?"

Change is a concept. The act of changing isn't instant, it's a *process*. The period during which this process happens is sometimes called "transition": the space between the old and the new.

Change is not just a beginning, it's an ending. Both letting go of the old and embracing the new are uncomfortable for people.

Transition is inherently confusing. Day-to-day life during the transition is complex. Each day is a combination of shutting down old work, engaging in special transition work, and beginning new work.

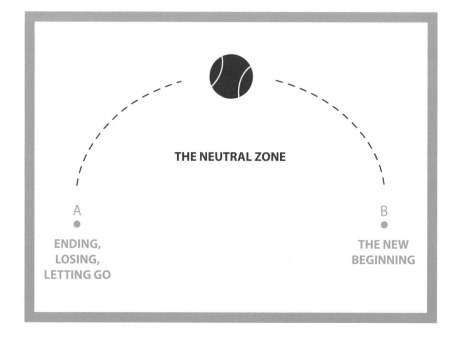

THE NEUTRAL ZONE

A
ENDING,
LOSING,
LETTING GO

B
THE NEW
BEGINNING

SO WHAT DO YOU DO IF YOU'VE BEEN ELECTED HEAD OF STATE— THE STATE OF CONFUSION, THAT IS?

Start simple. Get your key communicators together and fill out something like this:

WHAT WE KNOW	WHAT WE DON'T KNOW	WHEN WE WILL KNOW IT

Then have your communication team start carrying those messages to the organization, as appropriate. You can't avoid the state of confusion, but you can make it a nicer place to live.

YOUR TRANSITION TEAM

Next, identify the different groups you need to manage through the transition. Transition is a marathon, not a sprint, so think of it this way:

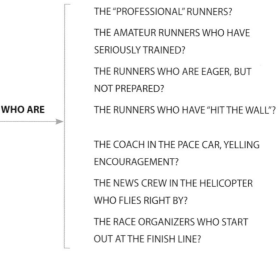

WHO ARE

THE "PROFESSIONAL" RUNNERS?

THE AMATEUR RUNNERS WHO HAVE
SERIOUSLY TRAINED?

THE RUNNERS WHO ARE EAGER, BUT
NOT PREPARED?

THE RUNNERS WHO HAVE "HIT THE WALL"?

THE COACH IN THE PACE CAR, YELLING
ENCOURAGEMENT?

THE NEWS CREW IN THE HELICOPTER
WHO FLIES RIGHT BY?

THE RACE ORGANIZERS WHO START
OUT AT THE FINISH LINE?

Different groups **need** different kinds of support. Different groups can **provide** different kinds of support. Understand who plays each role, so you can structure your transition team appropriately.

---

reference | Prosci, www.prosci.com

To learn more, see:
Bridges, William.
Managing Transitions: Making the Most of Change.
Da Capo Press, 2003.

People Prefer
the Predictable

The proof is in the potatoes. McDonald's would not be so popular if people preferred the unpredictable. So what's the appeal? The appeal is getting the same thing, every time. By choosing what is predictable, we are able to operate in automatic pilot and conserve our limited resources—time and energy— for things that we find meaningful. Confronted with something unpredictable on the horizon, we will fight for certainty, security, and control.

 Engage the Masses : pg 172

THE SOLUTION

MAKE YOUR CHANGE INITIATIVE PREDICTABLE.
BUT HOW CAN "CHANGE" BE PREDICTABLE?

Link it to what people know. Show them how it's similar to a previous and successful change. Draw comparisons to processes or companies they like. Use positive metaphors.

No surprises. Give people advance warning. Involve them. Tell them something during each step of the initiative. Advance information helps people plan for the change, giving them control.

Be specific. Ensure each individual understands exactly what the change will be like. If people can imagine their work lives after the change, they will get that comfortable, routine feeling earlier in the implementation.

HOW MUCH CONTROL DO WE HAVE OVER THE WEATHER? ZERO – YET, AN ENTIRE INDUSTRY HAS BEEN BUILT AROUND TRYING TO PREDICT IT. THOUGH OFTEN TOTALLY WRONG, THE PREDICTIONS GIVE US A FALSE SENSE OF CONTROL AND EXPECTATION – ENABLING US TO DEAL WITH CONSTANT CHANGE AND UNPREDICTABILITY.

We're Hardwired to Resist Change

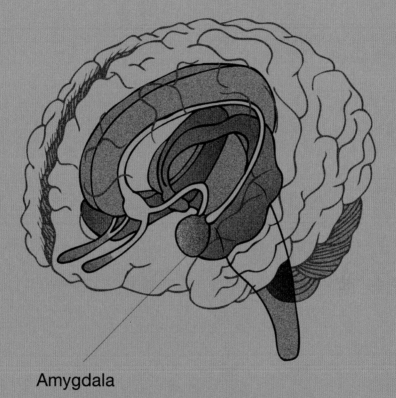

Amygdala

The brain determines
your emotional reaction

People are resistant to change because the amygdala, a part of the brain, interprets change as a threat to the body and releases the hormones of fear: fight or flight. The amygdala works to protect the body from change. This is why, when organizations announce a new change—even with many expected benefits— employees are likely to interpret the change as a threat and have an emotional reaction against it.

Learn More About Vision : pg 10

TO ADDRESS RESISTANCE, WE NEED TO OVERCOME THE PSYCHOLOGICAL COSTS OF CHANGE AND FOCUS ON:

- Dissatisfaction with the way things are now; change leaders most often forget to focus on this aspect

- Positive vision of the future

- Concrete steps to make the vision a reality.

GLEICHER'S FORMULA

D = Dissatisfaction with how things are

V = Vision of what is possible

F = First, concrete steps that can be taken towards the vision

R = Resistance

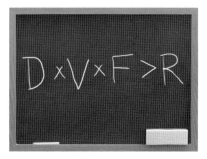

reference   Beckhard, Richard.
Organization Development: Strategies and Models.
Reading, MA: Addison-Wesley, 1969.
Also See David Gleicher.

Change Your Mind

NEURAL PATHWAYS IN THE BRAIN

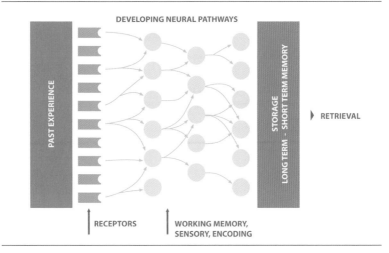

DEVELOPING NEURAL PATHWAYS

PAST EXPERIENCE

STORAGE
LONG TERM - SHORT TERM MEMORY

RETRIEVAL

RECEPTORS

WORKING MEMORY,
SENSORY, ENCODING

The path of least resistance

What do we do when faced with a new situation or experience? Naturally, we relate past experience to the new situation.

The brain develops neural pathways—physical folds and grooves—to connect concepts, knowledge, and past experience. What does this mean for changing people's behavior?

It is hard to break old pathways. **So, take the path of least resistance: relate new information to old.**

Engrain new information by **repeating it consistently and often.**

Involve new people and environments to surprise the brain—keep it from predicting what will happen next.

We Like Following Those Old Pathways : pg 85

A clean break

Sometimes the only way to change our minds is to break completely from those old habits. So why don't we? Old habits cut deep ruts through our brains, in the form of neural pathways. Building a new path takes a lot of effort and repetition.

When are we willing to go to all that trouble to learn a new way? When the current situation is unbearable.

♦ Describe what's wrong with now.

♦ Talk about the bad things that will happen if we continue on our current course.

♦ Help people see that the change will avoid the pain.

Clarifying the pain of now gets people moving. Now all we have to provide is a direction.

SECTION 5
Culture

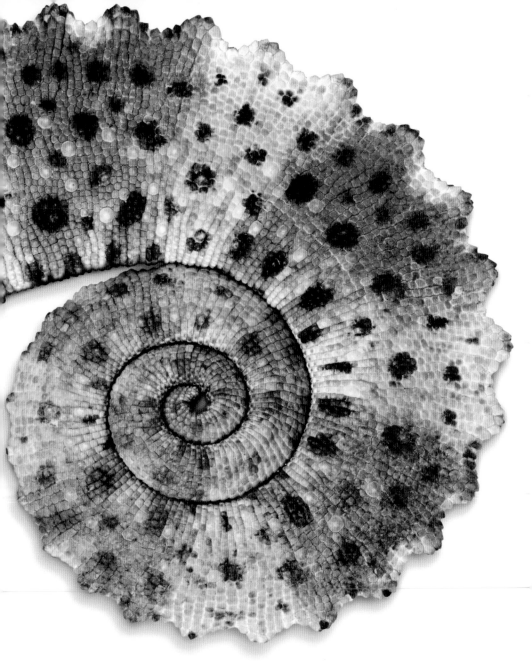

It's the Culture, Stupid!

"CULTURE EATS STRATEGY FOR BREAKFAST."

Mark Fields, Ford Motor Company

"Two of three transformation initiatives fail." That's according to a 2005 article in the Harvard Business Review. And it's a fairly conservative estimate; statistics and descriptions of failed change initiatives abound. Many researchers and analysts agree that the missing ingredient is strong change management, which can have a dramatic effect on ROI. And the very foundation of managing change is using the culture of the organization.

Culture is the immune system of an organization. Culture knows what the organization is; it knows what it's not. It attacks challengers and invaders and refuses to let them change the body. So why fight the very thing that protects the identity of your organization? Don't. Work with it.

But how can we harness culture?

First, by understanding it. Then, by plotting a course that plays to its strengths.

"In all chaos there is a cosmos,
in all disorder a secret order."

– CARL JUNG

One of the best ways to look at organizational culture
is through the lens of archetypes. Archetypes were first
defined by Carl Jung. While they have been present
throughout history, archetypes, in Jung's view, are more
than the stories we tell each other about heroism,
compassion, or achievement. Archetypes are innate,
universal models that can be used to predict behavior.

GIVE ME AN EXAMPLE

Conducting a workshop for the army? Don't start with a group hug. Maybe an obstacle course.

Communicating with nurses about a new drug formula? Don't call it, "Bottom Line Results." Save that for your banking client. Call it, "What this means to your patient."

Launching an initiative with a government agency? Lead with proven methods and results.

Managing change at Harley Davidson? Surprise them. They want to see how they're going to remain unique and revolutionary.

THESE ARE SOME ORGANIZATIONS AND THEIR TYPICAL ARCHETYPES.

ARMY → HERO
HOSPITAL → CAREGIVERS
BANK → SAGE
MOTORCYCLE CO. → REVOLUTIONARY
GOVERNMENT → EVERYMAN

HOW DO WE IDENTIFY OUR CULTURE?

Carol Pearson, PhD, has completed extraordinary work identifying active organizational culture. Her tools provide quantitative and qualitative analysis of an organization's core identity. Her research quantifies the presence of 12 universal archetypes that define:

♦ GROUP IDENTITY, PURPOSE, MEANING, AND MOTIVATION

♦ VALUES AND STRENGTHS

♦ OPERATING STYLE AND BEHAVIOR

♦ OPPORTUNITIES AND CHALLENGES

ORIENTATION	ARCHETYPE	CULTURE	EMPHASIS
Stability / Structure	Caregiver	Mission of mercy	Responding to needs, serving others, nurturance / stability
	Ruler	Royal court	Taking charge, sets standards, managing complex systems
	Creator	Artists' co-op	Generating ideas, designing forms / structures, creating products
Results / Achievement	Hero	Winning team	Achieving goals, overcoming obstacles, crusading for others
	Revolutionary	Band of rebels	Questioning status quo, taking risks, achieving breakthroughs
	Magician	Miracle workers	Seeing possibilities, embracing change, synchronicity
Community / Belonging	Jester	Playmates	Having fun, being clever / witty, brainstorming
	Every person	The gang	Banding together, democracy, surviving difficult times
	Lover	Beautiful people	Forming relationships, commitment, achieving consensus
Learning / Growth	Idealist	The happy family	Persevering cheerfully, sticking to the rules, keeping the faith
	Explorer	Caravan / outpost	Blazing new trails, taking individual initiatives, staying current
	Sage	Laboratory	Thinking things through, building expertise, gathering information

Source: Summarized from Pearson, Carol S. *Archetypes in Organizational Settings: A Client's Guide to the OTCI™ Professional Report*. Gainesville, FL: CAPT, 2003. Used by permission.

VALUES	HELPS PEOPLE	BRAND
Service, care, altruism, compassion, selflessness, sacrifice for greater good	Find care / support / nurturance; feel compassion / kindness	Campbell's Soup
Power, control, order, reputation, social responsibility, leadership	Take charge, become leaders, gain power / prestige	American Express
Imagination, innovation, expression, design, aesthetics, good taste	Express themselves or their imaginations, invent / design / build	General Electric
Courage, energy, focus, discipline, principled action, giving your all	Overcome obstacles / win, crusade for others	Nike
Risk, radical thinking, non-conformity, liberation, outrageousness	Take risks / achieve breakthroughs, challenge status quo	Harley Davidson
Intuition, vision, inspiration, self-awareness, intention, transformation	Transform / realize dreams, see possibilities	Disney
Playfulness, thinking outside the box, living in the moment, resourcefulness	Enjoy / experience the moment, be clever / witty / ingenious	Miller Lite
Fairness, reciprocity, camaraderie, honesty, democracy, equality, pride	Fit in / be ok just as they are, build community / band together	Wal-Mart
Closeness, openness, beauty, living life to the fullest, enthusiasm	Find love or bliss, live life to fullest	Hallmark
Loyalty, goodness, optimism, perseverance, faith, allegiance to shared goals	Renew / refresh / enjoy simple pleasures, live shared ideals / values	McDonald's
Individuality, independence, new experiences, growth, self-actualization	Experience freedom, adventure, blaze / pioneer new trails	National Geographic
Intelligence, truth, objectivity, insight, knowledge, critical thinking	Understand the world, gain insight / wisdom	Discovery

references

Sirkin, Harold L., Perry Keenan and Alan Jackson. "The Hard Side of Change Management." *Harvard Business Review,* October 2005.

Petouhoff, Natalie, Tamra, Chandler, and Beth Montag-Schultz, "The Business Impact of Change Management: What Is the Common / Denominator for High Project ROIs?" *Graziado Business Report,* 9, no. 3 (2006) http://gbr.pepperdine.edu/063/change.html

Fields, Mark, "Culture Eats Strategy for Breakfast." From McCracken, Jeffrey. "'Way Forward' Requires Culture Shift At Ford." *Wall Street Journal, January 23, 2006.*
p. B1

To learn more, see:
Corlett, John G. and Carol S., Pearson
Mapping the Organizational Psyche: A Jungian Theory of Organizational Dynamics and Change.
Gainesville, FL: CAPT, 2003.

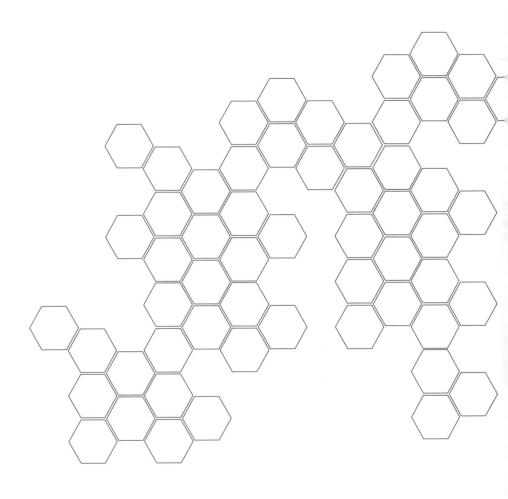

Subculture Savvy

Structuring change for subcultures

Change professionals know we must consider culture when managing change. Culture is powerful. If we do our jobs right, it works for the change, not against it.

But it's not that simple. Within the organization lies a teeming microcosm of subcultures. An organization is alive with the various norms and rules of individual teams and departments. Each group has a different standard for successful behavior and performance.

> "Apple is a culture of revolutionaries. I work here because I 'think different.' On the other hand, I am a professional accountant. My department values routine, dependability, accuracy, and conformance to standard. So I might wear flip-flops to the office, but my work is strictly 'business attire.'"

Change plans must address the complexity of multiple cultures: both the organization AND department. Employees affiliate with both. To reach them, the change plan must harness both cultural identities.

> "I love it! This change will help us 'think different' better! Predictably! I really like predictability. Count me in."

And you wonder why change is complex....

Different cultures have different norms, and therefore different behaviors. Behavioral norms and subcultures vary at the following levels:

- ◆ Organization
- ◆ Business Unit
- ◆ Geography
- ◆ Department
- ◆ Job
- ◆ Individual

DEPARTMENT	ARCHETYPE
IT	*Hero*	"If Accounting can't close the books by cutover, I'll do it myself… even if it takes all night!"
Sales	*Magician*	"Watch me generate results! Whoa. Did you see that?"
Research and Development	*Sage*	"We've studied this for years. And it's likely the result you want can be achieved… If our hypothesis is correct. Let me look at your goals in detail."
Ops	*Everyperson*	"We're in this together and we need all hands to make this work. Have the right people been involved?"

Now, how do we construct a change plan for this?

A large oil company hired a strategy firm to recommend a new organization structure. Five consultants worked from a conference room for months, periodically emerging for interviews and data collection. While their recommendations were sound, the organization battled them because, as an Everyperson organization, they didn't trust the result. The employees felt people were not appropriately involved.

Successful change managers learn about cultural archetypes, assess the archetypes in the organization, and act with culture in mind. Here are some examples:

STRUCTURE PROJECT TEAMS

- Cultures that might require larger teams and more representation/participation include: Caregiver, Creator, Magician, Jester, Everyperson, Lover, and Idealist.

- Cultures that can accommodate tighter more efficient teams include: Ruler, Hero, Revolutionary, Explorer, and Sage.

The project team is the "first impression" of the change itself. It's a data point people use as they judge whether the change is good or bad—who participated? How were they chosen? What was their role? Constructing a team consistent with the culture signals that the change is positive. What happens when change professionals ignore subcultures?

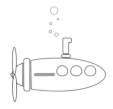

CREATE A WORKPLAN AND SCHEDULE

- Ruler cultures indicate short timelines, and fewer people.

- Everyperson/Caregiver archetypes lend themselves to larger teams and more frequent meetings, as more people need to be involved.

Understanding this up front can help you manage expectations. People view ability to meet timelines as an indicator of change success.

Approach the activities in the change model—**STRATEGY, INTERNALIZATION, FOCUS** and **SUSTAINABILITY**—differently based on the culture.

DESIGN THE CHANGE EFFORTS

♦ Present the change Strategy to a Creator organization, emphasizing how the end state helps generate better ideas.

♦ Internalization for a Sage organization might incorporate many opportunities to review supporting research, listening to expert speakers, and conducting analysis as part of the deployment process.

♦ For a Revolutionary culture, try to Focus attention on the new behaviors by physically destroying the old report printers to make room for online reporting.

♦ Sustainability for a Hero culture might include intense competition during training exercises, whereas the Sage might do better with learner-directed solutions.

Shape the stakeholders' experience to build evidence that the change will be successful, and do it in a way that feels true to them. This helps stakeholders feel confident taking another step forward. Once they do, they feel confident stepping forward again. And those repeated successful steps forward result in lasting organizational change.

SECTION 6
Branding

Brand With Caution

The golden arches. The Nike swoosh. The Apple… (with the bite taken out, of course, to show their rebel side).

All of these are fine examples of branding. When companies have products with which consumers can easily identify, brands become legendary.

Branding is not just for products or cattle anymore though; many company projects and change initiatives are now branded. To make sure your brand has the impact you want, pay attention to two things: the process and the pitfalls.

 Does Your Brand Fit Your Culture : pg 98
Use the Right Symbols : pg 124

The Good

WHEN A PROJECT'S NAME OR LOGO REFLECTS WHAT IS BEING DONE OR WHAT IT WILL MEAN TO END USERS.

Unify

This company values community, shared sacrifice, collaboration, and collective success. The project is an ERP implementation which will help all their systems and processes work seamlessly together.

This is a science and technology firm. They see themselves as intellectuals and value rigor and excellence above all else. The project is to develop a business readiness team meeting space; a place to innovate and to hash out new ideas and issues that interfere with performance.

This company considers themselves an elite group, where indiviual accomplishment is expected and celebrated. The project is a reorganization and system upgrade, prompted by some severe shifts in the company's market. They're fighting to retain their market share and stay alive. The project has aggressive deadlines; project team leaders are charged with firing up the "troops" and working intensely until they go live.

The Bad

DON'T MAKE IT BORING!

"Business Success 2007" doesn't say anything.

"IT Upgrade" or "SAP Connect" are strategies, not visions.

The Ugly

DON'T BE MEANINGLESS, OUT OF TOUCH, AND/OR TOO CLEVER OR EXUBERANT.

"Go for the Gold 2008!"

"Starship Synergy"

"The Tiger Team Initiative"

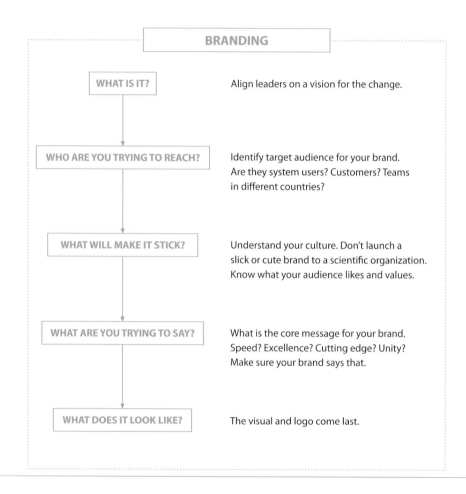

BRANDING

| WHAT IS IT? | Align leaders on a vision for the change. |

| WHO ARE YOU TRYING TO REACH? | Identify target audience for your brand. Are they system users? Customers? Teams in different countries? |

| WHAT WILL MAKE IT STICK? | Understand your culture. Don't launch a slick or cute brand to a scientific organization. Know what your audience likes and values. |

| WHAT ARE YOU TRYING TO SAY? | What is the core message for your brand. Speed? Excellence? Cutting edge? Unity? Make sure your brand says that. |

| WHAT DOES IT LOOK LIKE? | The visual and logo come last. |

reference | http://ezinearticles.com/?A-Brief-History-of-Branding&id=817828

To learn more, see:
http://www.paramountbooks.com/beyond-
mission-statement?keyword=beyond

Symbols Matter

A symbol is a token

It stands for something else.

A symbol is not a brand

Brands are carefully developed to incorporate culture, psychology, and marketing principles.

A symbol matters

Symbols and symbolic gestures evoke strong emotion, and that's a powerful tool.

YOU TAKE THE CAKE

An independently owned company hosted a monthly birthday party for employees. The birthday cake was symbolic of caring and team spirit. An international Fortune 500 company acquired the small firm and wanted to cut costs. They ended the cake celebrations. Now the company had a new symbol. Every month, the party date came and went, reminding people of the impersonal, bottom-line ethos of the holding company. For years thereafter, "the cake" was the symbol for happy times before the acquisition. Employees made jokes like, "This company takes the cake." and "You can't have your cake and work here too."

SAFETY FIRST

Safety and caring are the core values of this major energy company. Literally every meeting begins with a "safety moment" where each employee shares a safe or unsafe experience they observed that week. Every day, people pile out of their cubes for a group "stretch break." Work stations have a tool that locks up computers for three minutes so employees can look away from the screens and rest their eyes. Near every door are antibacterial lotions and tissues, to prevent illness. Employees back into parking spaces and confront anyone they catch driving while on the phone. Over the top? No. These symbolic objects and activities focus attention on the behaviors they want: constant awareness of risk and preventing injury on all levels.

"Symbols give regularity, unity, and
systematics to the practices of a group."

– FRENCH SOCIOLOGIST, PIERRE BOURDIEU

SYMBOLS

VARY BY ORGANIZATION AND PROJECT. They must fit the culture of the organization and the initiative at hand.

MUST BE UNDERSTOOD TO BE SUCCESSFUL. Choose a symbol or symbolic gesture that you're sure people will "get." Stay away from those that might have a dual or unintended meaning. You might need to frame the symbol, at the outset, with images or language that helps people understand your message.

SHOULD BE CAREFULLY CHOSEN. Ask, watch, listen, and take notes. Notice the stories on the grapevine—often existing symbols hold the story together. Identified a potential new symbol? Test it with a few stakeholders to see if there are hidden hot-buttons or cultural pitfalls.

ARE ESPECIALLY IMPORTANT IN CERTAIN CASES. If your initiative is about merging, acquiring, or outsourcing, those efforts evoke strong emotions. Choosing the right symbols or symbolic gestures can cast the effort in the right light.

CAN BE LAYERED. Use more universal symbols, as needed, to tie your initiative to a bigger picture, like company mission or global and cultural trends.

USE SYMBOLS

♦ During project branding, when you determine your message, name, logo, graphics, and stories

♦ In project communications, both internal and external

♦ Whenever you have a project event (kick-off, change agent session, team-building, celebration)

♦ In the design of your solution (on-screen graphics, icons, models).

Combating
Existing Symbols

If we want to change people's actions, we must focus attention on the new behavior.

WATCH OUT FOR THE SUCKER PUNCH

Your biggest opponent in this match: the symbols reinforcing the old behavior.

An IT department within a private hospital near Chicago was collapsing under the weight of "Yes!" That's how they defined customer service: "Always say 'yes!'" The fifteen-person team was buried, delivered projects chronically late, and spent hours on low-priority tasks. To meet all their commitments, they needed to increase their headcount to 250.

To combat this issue, they implemented a formal project approval process, allowing the team to prioritize and deliver the truly strategic projects. The problem? Everyone in the hospital had the pager number for his or her favorite IT person. Those pagers weren't just communication devices. They were symbols of direct access, personal relationships, and premier service.

From the IT point of view, the ideal solution was to eliminate pagers and have employees call one number to enter requests, which would then be prioritized. But the pagers were such a powerful symbol that no one wanted to give them up! So IT reassigned phone numbers; this symbolized the beginning of a new process.

ACTIVITY

Draw a line connecting the symbol to the behavior it **undermines.**

SEPARATE BUILDINGS		ACTING
CLOSED DOORS		COLLABORATING
SIGNATURES		PARTICIPATING
BLACKBERRIES		COMMUNICATING

Answers: Closed Doors = Communicating; Blackberries = Participating; Signatures = Acting; Separate Buildings = Collaborating

Draw a line connecting the symbol to the behavior it **promotes.**

BIRTHDAY CAKES		SHARING
OPEN SPACE		BRAINSTORMING
SLICK TECHNOLOGY		CONNECTING
WHITEBOARD WALLS		INNOVATING

Answers: Open Space = Sharing; Birthday Cakes = Connecting; Whiteboard Walls = Brainstorming; Slick Technology = Innovating

SECTION 7
Communication

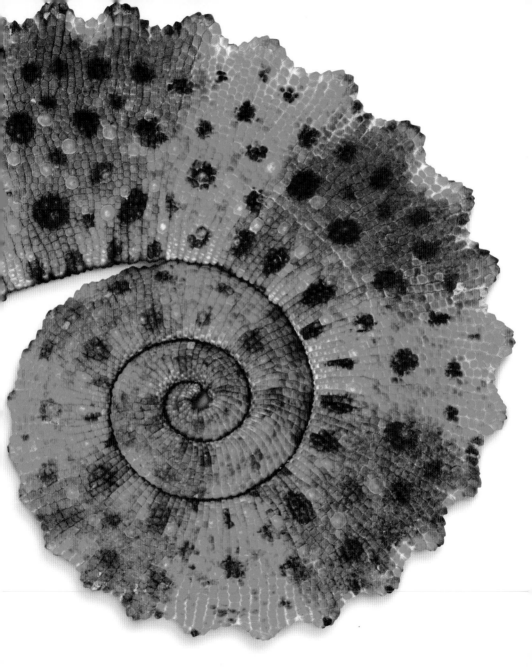

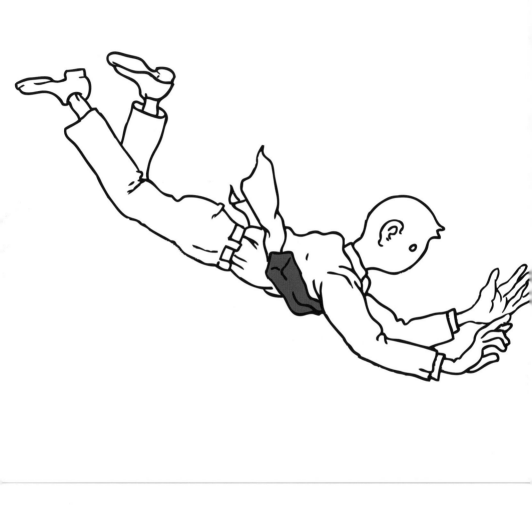

Change
Communication
101

What's so different about **change** communication?

Change communication has to address the unique state that characterizes a group in transition: Being in between, uncertain, without familiar comforts or landmarks, in motion from one place to another.

> "It's not so much that we're afraid of change or so in love with the old ways, but it's that place in between that we fear... It's like being between trapezes. It's Linus when his blanket is in the dryer. There's nothing to hold on to."
>
> – MARILYN FERGUSON

COMMUNICATION BASICS

1. **Focus on the magic combination for each communication.**

   The right target audience with the right message.

2. **Repeat, reiterate, and reinforce.**

   Studies show that your audience needs to experience your
   message seven to ten times before they really get it. Don't
   assume that they're paying attention the first six times!

3. **Use third party validation when possible.**

   Make sure communication source/quotes are not always
   from you, but from someone influential. Instant credibility.

4. **Use human examples and real numbers.**

   Examples and numbers help the message "stick." Do you
   remember "Where's the beef?" Do you know how many dentists
   recommend sugarless gum? Of course you do.

A NEW COMMUNICATION BASIC—THE PUSH AND PULL

Push or Pain Force: The pain of maintaining the status quo. This is a force that can push people in many directions. The feeling is, "I don't care where I go, just get me out of here!"

Pull or Remedy Force: The pleasure of achieving or anticipating a desired outcome. This is a force that pulls people in one direction—the direction that you are providing. The feeling is, "I want to be there!"

Too often, change communication focuses only on the remedy. But then there is no balance. The remedy has no basis without the pain. Pain is the "why?" All change communication must include both pain and remedy: the push and the pull.

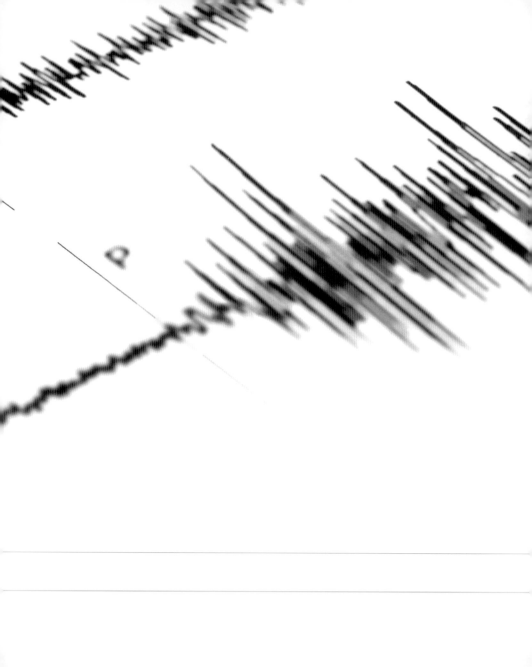

The Big Shift

From project initiation through go-live, your audience focus shifts from sponsors and executives to end-users. And your message evolves from the project to the solution.

EXAMPLE OF A COMMUNICATION STRATEGY FOR IT PROJECTS

PROJECT PHASE

AUDIENCE		PLAN ▶	DESIGN ▶
LEADERSHIP ▼	COMMUNICATION GOALS	Build awareness of case for change Solidify support for project	Grow understanding Develop buy-in for solution
	VEHICLES	Project message Project presentation / business case	Status meetings and presentations Demo/status road shows Preview project website
PROJECT TEAM ▼	COMMUNICATION GOALS	Engage and mobilize team Align project message Ensure understanding of roles and responsibilities	Sustain momentum Ensure alignment between teams and business
	VEHICLES	Team meetings Project message	Team meetings Project website
USERS ▼	COMMUNICATION GOALS		Build awareness
	VEHICLES		Super-user network Project website
ALL EMPLOYEES ■	COMMUNICATION GOALS		Build awareness
	VEHICLES		Project-focused email Newsletter article Cascaded communications

TEST ▶	GO LIVE ■
Ease transition concerns Build momentum for pilot	Prepare for go-live Advocate solution
Solution message Solution demo Pilot plan presentation	Training Launch updates
Overcome resistance Build momentum for launch	Prepare for launch Celebrate and encourage
Deployment team role requirements Test status Solution message	Executive email Launch updates and tips Reward and recognition tools
Grow understanding of solution Generate buy-in for launch	Prepare for go-live Encourage to adopt
Solution demo/training Deployment plan communication Message from executive(s)	Training Go-live user meetings Super-user updates and tips
Sustain awareness	Grow understanding
Solution-focused newsletter article	Launch email Employee meetings FAQ document

Consider what people need to hear, and when. Your communication should evolve as your project moves forward.

Not Communicating Is Communicating

You never get a second chance to make a first impression. Yeah, it sounds like a '70s shampoo commercial, but it's true! There are good reasons to hold off on saying certain things. But if you hold off communicating for too long, you are telling them something. You just don't realize it.

WHY ARE YOU NOT COMMUNICATING?

- ☐ The sponsors aren't all on board yet and you're afraid to say something they won't like.
- ☐ Implementation is such a long way away. "You'll get to that later."
- ☐ You haven't figured out exactly what the change looks like yet.
- ☐ You don't have people in place to deliver the messages.
- ☐ You don't want to start a panic about what might happen.
- ☐ You're not staffed and ready for questions that you might get once you open the conversation.

WHAT ARE YOU COMMUNICATING BY NOT COMMUNICATING?

+ There's something to fear.

+ The project doesn't have the support of sponsors or managers.

+ The project team is poorly organized and poorly led.

+ "They" don't care about how this might impact "me."

+ The change might not happen at all.

WHAT SHOULD YOU COMMUNICATE, IF YOU'RE NOT READY FOR THE BIG KICK-OFF?

+ Problems with the status quo—the case for change.

+ Short quotes from executive sponsors on why the change is needed.

+ Spotlight pieces on individual project team members.

+ The origin of the initiative's name.

+ Success stories from other organizations that implemented something similar.

+ A broad timeline for the change.

+ How this project fits with other corporate initiatives.

+ When you will share more information.

I Already Told Them!

"Of course everyone in the organization knows about (*check one*)

- ❑ our new system."
- ❑ our reorganization."
- ❑ our product launch."
- ❑ our _____ (*insert initiative name here*)"

"I told them (*check one*)

- ❑ at the all-hands meeting."
- ❑ in the memo."
- ❑ on our website."
- ❑ at the off-site."
- ❑ in that one email."

"So why are they (*check one*)

- ❑ asking so many questions?"
- ❑ starting rumors?"
- ❑ ignoring our requests for input?"
- ❑ not preparing for the change?"
- ❑ saying they have no idea what's going on?"

Sound familiar?
What's the solution?

Repeat It

Once is not enough. People go through stages: exposure, awareness, attention, retention, and action. By the time you and your team can deliver the message in your sleep, your audience is just starting to get it. Repeat, repeat, repeat!

Layer It

Deliver the same information in different ways. This gives you the repetition you need and a better chance of having it "stick." Different people are receptive to different methods. Some are visual, some like data, and some need the interaction of a question-and-answer session or the power of a demonstration.

Share It

Let others help deliver your message, adding their own perspective. Nothing succeeds like local angles and human stories. Enlist others to tell your story, sing your praises, and get your message out. Third parties also lend credibility to your project.

Test It

Don't just assume people know; find out. Have managers or change agents ask people what they know about the initiative. Start one of your info sessions with a little quiz. Ask people to write down their understanding of the project's purpose, or the wildest rumor they've heard. Collect data from your website or emails to find out who's visiting or reading. Then you'll know where you stand.

Be Willing
to Say the
Hard Things

Most change involves good news and bad news

The good news:

- A thriving business
- More efficiency
- Response to a crisis or market conditions
- Improved bottom line
- Increased compensation
- Job security
- Better relationships with customers
- More pleasant work environment.

The bad news:

- Reorganization
- New skills to learn
- New priorities
- Possible layoffs
- Increased workload in the short term
- Periods of confusion and uncertainty
- Loss of process and systems that are familiar.

Spreading the good news is easy. The bad news is another story.

WHY TALK ABOUT THE BAD NEWS?

Because discomfort is a catalyst for change.

Your target audience will understand more clearly the need for change. Clarity means they'll be more likely to support it and less likely to resist it.

Acting on their own, people will make better decisions if they have better information.

Credibility builds trust. Trust helps when you need your target audience to do something to support the project.

Accurate information fights misinformation. Minimize rumors and distractions by making it clear that your team has the answers.

It's the right thing to do. It's honest. It's fair. People deserve to know about the change that will affect their work lives.

We don't want negative reactions. We don't want dissent or resistance or defections. So why can't we just focus on the good news?

Most people can see through spin and hype. Build trust in the overall communication effort by telling it straight.

Communication Gotchas

WHEN

Are you too early? Are you saying things you're not sure about yet? Is it too late? Have people already drawn their own conclusions and moved on without you? Is your timing unfortunate?

A message sent just before a weekend or holiday will get lost. And if you don't coordinate with other major organizational happenings, your message will get swamped or trumped. A bonus, lay-off, day off, or regime change defeats your project news.

WHERE

Are you missing opportunities? What are the regular events for your audience? Meetings? Email updates? Websites?

Are you considering all the options? Where do people spend their informal worktime? Breakroom? Company gym? Chat rooms or communities? Be where they are. And bring your message.

HOW

Does the method fit the audience? Posters don't work for home-based workers. Blogs, websites, and chat rooms are useless for factory floor workers.

Do existing tools work? If not, create new ones, even for the life of the project.

Are you putting too much faith in existing methods? So there's a newsletter. Does anyone read it? And there's a website. How many hits does it get? From whom? Find out the effectiveness of those channels.

WHO

Do you have the right messenger? Not every executive has the respect or attention of your stakeholder group. Make sure your messenger is influential and charismatic.

How many people are in your target audience? Where are they located? What are their demographics, common interests, common experiences, and common dislikes? Draw on these to create a connection.

Are you using the right levels? Start with your intended audience. Who manages them? Who leads them? Who do they trust? Make a map of your audience to ensure that each group is covered by the right messenger.

WHAT

Are you communicating what's relevant to the audience? Too often, sponsors want to communicate strategy or vision, which can be overwhelming, "fluffy," and off-target. Start with your audience. Figure out what they need to know, then consider what you want to tell them.

Is communication the right solution? Think about the ultimate goal of the communication effort. If it's a change in behaviors or job skills, consider using a learning or training solution instead.

SECTION 8
Momentum

The Tipping Point

To make change happen, we must enlist the people of the organization. But who and how many?

First, determine the:

Critical Mass: the percentage of the organization that must respond and act to turn the organization in a new direction. Is it 20 percent? 50 percent? Should we involve all departments? All levels?

Identities of those who give the right energy to the change. External stakeholders? Who are the "influencers"? Who might live in a potential pocket of resistance?

IF THE MASS OF THE ORGAN-
IZATION IS CREATING THE
CHANGE PLAN, WHAT IS THE
CHANGE MANAGER'S ROLE?
COACH AND FACILITATOR —
THE ONE WHO TAKES THEM
THROUGH THE PROCESS OF
CRAFTING THE PLAN.

THERE'S NO ONE RIGHT ANSWER—IT'S DRIVEN BY THE NATURE OF THE ORGANIZATION.

TRY THESE METHODS:

- Brainstorm with some key people—those who know the organization and understand the change.

- Use visuals. Create a map of the organization's people and departments, identifying targets for involvement in the change. Are you covering the right areas? Are there any individuals you definitely want on board? Are all impacted groups represented?

- Look at previous initiatives. Who was involved? How did it go? Any lessons learned?

Let's say you've determined a need to involve 25 percent of the employees to create momentum and move the organization. Who are the best advocates for each stakeholder group and for the change? Choose representatives that cover all key areas.

YOUR RESULTS

These are the people who should actively participate in developing the change solution.

Put them in the same room. At the same time. Working on the same problem. Together.

- They will work through the change curve together.

- They will coach and support each other.

- They will self-correct the loud dissenters.

- They will craft a solution that actually works in their setting.

And when they leave, they will have a shared understanding of the desired state.

A major government agency was about to deploy a new IT system. This impacted over 50 locations across the United States and approximately 60,000 employees. It also represented a significant change in how the agency worked.

The change strategy: they identified representatives from all levels at each office (about 1,500 people in total) who participated in three-day change plan workshops, 200 people at a time. They worked in small groups and, through a facilitated process, created plans and shared ideas that sharpened each other's change strategies. When they left, the entire organization agreed upon a clear and consistent picture of what was to be done and how.

Five major companies from IT and defense sectors merged and centralized their human resources administrative processes. The resulting group assembled 100 people representing all levels and all companies who had a stake in the final design to create a shared service that worked across all companies. They met over three days, and, through a facilitated working session, generated a new organization design complete with overarching work processes, an impact analysis, and an initial deployment plan.

The result: Everyone agreed on overall roles/responsibilities and operations that could be refined with little iteration.

To learn more, see:
Dannemiller, Kathleen D. and Robert W. Jacobs.
"Changing the Way Organizations Change: A Revolution of Common Sense."
The Journal of Applied Behavioral Science
28, no (4) (1992): 480-498.

Don't Be Afraid
to Engage
the Masses

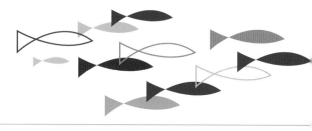

There is wisdom in crowds. Use the power of a large group to answer questions, poke holes in the plan, challenge the assumptions and identify ways to overcome barriers.

WHY?

It becomes their baby. When people feel heard, they are more likely to buy into the solution, even if they didn't agree with it in the first place.

It builds momentum. When you engage a large group at once, everyone leaves the room with a common understanding. And they will talk to their friends. You've effectively blitzed the organization.

Remember That Not Communicating Is Communicating : pg 147

The Psychology
of Signing On

We are hard-wired for self-preservation and therefore experts at assessing whether a new strategy, product, technology, or skill threatens or enhances our ability to thrive.

We do not endorse this new state until we know it's safe.

Change managers must create that psychologically safe place by engineering success early and often. Provide the clues people will read and use to construct a positive and compelling story.

For each stakeholder group:

♦ Identify interventions that will provide those positive elements.

♦ Lay them out on a timeline.

♦ Roll them out to orchestrate success.

Familiar

Acquaint them with what the change will be like. Use comparisons and first-hand experience. A wonderfully effective way to make change "friendly" is to compare the change to something the stakeholder knows and considers safe.

Example | For a major reorganization, reference another company who successfully reorganized. It's ok to look outside your industry. When a major pharmaceutical company wanted to implement a new quality process, they pointed to Apple as their role model.

To create first-hand experience, provide opportunities for stakeholders to "play" with the change. Generate business simulations and in-basket exercises to give people a taste of what the new work process feels like. Create snapshots of the live system so people can look at the screens, practice, and correct mistakes. This puts stakeholders at ease and builds a psychological pattern of performance that will come in handy when it's the real deal.

Controlled

Allow people to make decisions within the change experience. While some elements might not be negotiable, there are often tasks or deliverables where stakeholders can contribute. If that truly is not an option, simply providing information or a timeline when facts will be available provides the same relief.

Successful

Rather than a "big bang," orchestrate a "slow drip." Find a few low-risk elements of the final solution to share with stakeholders. Present them in a periodic and thoughtfully paced manner up to "go-live." First, show one user interface. Then a few solid reports. Then a "sandbox system." Make sure you build in opportunities for discussion and feedback with the project team. With each event, you'll find growing support for the subsequent event. And if all goes according to plan, the actual cut-over will feel so familiar, it's forgettable.

CONTROL EXAMPLE:

DURING A SIGNIFICANT MERGER, LAYOFFS AT A MAJOR DEFENSE COMPANY WERE NOT NEGOTIABLE. HOWEVER, THE COMPANY CREATED A SENSE OF CONTROL BY PROVIDING "PERSONAL CHANGE PLANS," WITH RESOURCES INDIVIDUALS COULD USE TO DETERMINE THEIR NEXT STEPS. IN IT INCLUDED TRAINING OPTIONS, OPEN POSITION DESCRIPTIONS, UPDATED ORGANIZATION CHARTS, TIMELINES, INTERNAL CONTACTS, AND A WORKSHEET FOR PLANNING "NEXT STEPS."

Once upon a time...

Emotion: It's All in the Story

"We are introducing a new product, carrot juice, in October. Training will be available this month. Any questions?"

-OR-

"Fifty years ago, we were the **only game in town**. Our founders came to California looking for the perfect place to grow carrots, and determined that Bakersfield offered a breathtaking opportunity—perfect climate, fertile soil, and a smart and determined workforce. As you know, our founders came in and created the market. And we dominated that market for fifty productive years.

But then the **market turned**. A competitor started fifteen miles from where we are, driving down prices, and taking market share. Our customers began to leave, and our jobs were threatened. Three years ago we realized, if we don't do something immediately, we would be finished.

So we began to **diversify**. First, we developed baby carrots—by simply carving larger carrots into smaller shapes, we found a convenience market for children, snacks, and entertainment. Then, we created the organic market. By packaging carrots in bulk with their greens, we could reduce packaging cost while appealing to customers looking for more of a farmer's market experience.

And now we are ready to launch **another exciting product** to the market: carrot juice! This product is a natural extension of our brand. It has a longer shelf life, which increases our distribution capability and reduces our inventory. It broadens our consumer base to include the thirsty as well as the hungry. It uses the inventory we might not be able to sell otherwise. In short, this highly profitable product continues to ensure the stability of our company and jobs for ourselves, our children, and our grandchildren.

Of course, a new product means that **we'll all have to learn** to market it, produce it, and get it to our customers. We'll start walking everyone through the new processes on Thursday."

Which has the most impact?
Same point, but the second taps into people's emotions about the company.

Emotion cements learning and compels people to change. It is a powerful tool. Facts flit in and out of our brains. But we are more apt to remember facts connected to emotions. This is why politicians talk about Joe the Plumber and Rosa Parks, and why you remember the make and model of your first love's car. These messages and facts, embedded in emotional content, stay with the listener. If the organization's people associate the change with a positive, powerful emotion, your change cannot be stopped.

So what's the best way to engage emotion?

Tell a compelling story. Stories capture imagination because they grip our emotion. And if a story resonates, it's wildfire.

Storytelling has a methodology. You can reliably repeat successful storytelling. With apologies to professional storytellers and Gustav Freytag, here's how:

1	**Define the point of the story:** What do you want to prove?	We need to launch a new product: Carrot juice. This new product will be good for us.
2	**Identify the hero (protagonist) and what that person desires.** We are drawn to real people, particularly those with passion, obsession, and flaws. (*Note: Feel free to think of the company as the person.*)	Hero—our founders and our company Desire—grow and sell carrots!
3	**Determine the conflicts the hero must overcome to get what she wants.** These conflicts should start small and increase exponentially. The speed at which the conflicts occur determines pace and your audience's interest!	Conflict: market turned Conflict: new competitor Conflict: customers leave, jobs threatened
4	**Determine the climax.** The climax is the decision the hero must make at the point of no return. The hero cannot go back to the status quo.	Diversify!
5	**Describe the result.** The untangling of the knot, or dénouement, is how everyone winds up at the end—how the story is resolved.	Baby carrots, organic carrots, and now juice.
6	**Call to action.** OK, that's not actually part of storytelling, but it is when you're using storytelling to create momentum for change. Now that you have everyone emotionally engaged, get them to act!	Take training!

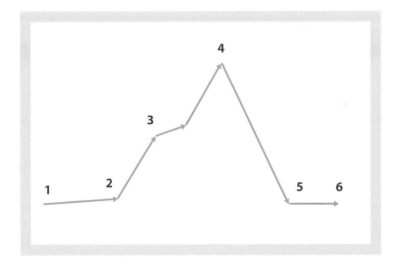

Storytelling is about pace and emotion. Getting people to care. If you craft a good story about your change, you gain the organization's heart, attention, and motivation to move.

Map It

When it comes to orchestrating change, pace is everything. A Change Map can help you ensure people get the right experiences in a timely manner, no stakeholder group is overlooked, and no one gets inundated. It's also critical to organizing your own team's efforts.

A CHANGE MAP CAN BRING FORTH AWARENESS
THAT WOULD OTHERWISE GO UNNOTICED.

All stakeholder groups: And the unique experiences you plan for them. Adjust the number of these experiences based on the importance and degree of the change to the organization.

Major project milestones: Change activities should increase before and after these.

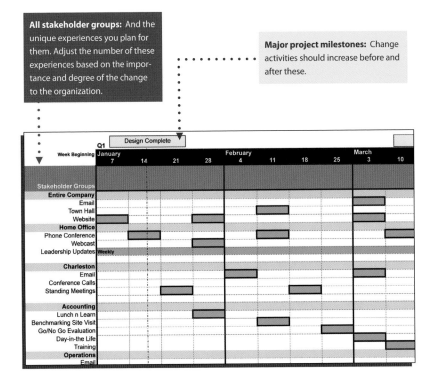

► March 5th is a bad week. Can the project team handle this?

► Look at the stakeholder's experience. Is anyone overwhelmed? Does it feel appropriate given everything else each stakeholder group might be experiencing?

189

Stakeholders
Get Weary

And when they get weary....

NOT TOO LONG

Behavioral scientists studying people taking vacations found that we don't actually enjoy a long vacation. After a short time, we adapt to it and take it for granted. We do enjoy anticipating and remembering it, but we only remember the particularly intense experiences—good or bad. We also remember whom we vacation with.

ANTICIPATE

COMPANIONS

INTENSITY!

Further, our enjoyment is enhanced if the vacation is interrupted by "normal life" and then we are allowed to return to fun and leisure. Therefore, best case scenario is coupling an intense experience (peak) with an interruption (end), to break that vacation up (partition).

COMBINATION OF INTENSE AND NOT TOO LONG, WITH BREAKS

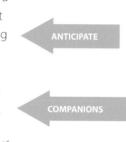

One might argue that organizational change is no vacation; however, these principles can help when creating a change management experience for our stakeholders. How about building in the following:

- Anticipation
- Intensity
- High points
- Breaks and deadlines
- Novelty and variation (novelty supports "intense" and variation creates "breaks")
- Group interaction—where the individuals already like each other

THE NOTION OF PEAK-END EXPERIENCES HAS INTERESTING IMPLICATIONS FOR TRAINING. LEARNERS MIGHT BE BETTER SERVED BY SHORTER, PERIODIC TRAINING SESSIONS RATHER THAN A SIX-WEEK BOOT CAMP.

To learn more, see:
Bennett, Drake.
"The Best Vacation Ever."
The Boston Globe (Boston, MA)
June 20, 2010.
http://www.boston.com/bostonglobe/ideas/articles/2010/06/20/the_best_vacation_ever/

SECTION 9
Measurement

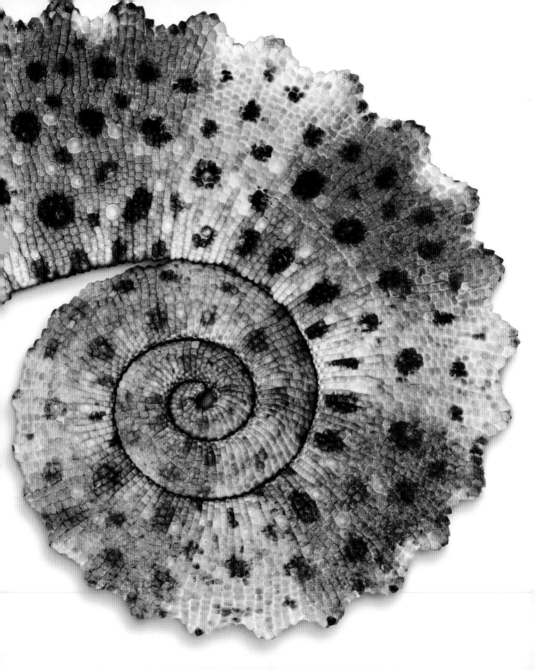

If a "change" happens in the woods, and no one measured it, did it really happen?

Top executives and project sponsors usually want to know whether the change was successful.

How do you tell? Because you stayed on-budget? By the quiet after the storm? Think again.

During the planning phase

WHAT | Agree on what success *is*. That's what you measure.

HOW | Agree on the metrics you will use and how you will collect and analyze data.

WHEN | Build in checkpoints for measurement. Budget time to measure and react to results.

WHAT | **Agree on what success *is*. That's what you measure.**

What should we measure?

♦ Refer to the mission, the project charter, and the business case. What did they say about goals and success?

♦ Measure sponsorship, team efficiency, and team performance.

♦ Measure progress toward business goals.

♦ Measure how well you navigated those rocky waters—things like mitigating the disruption to your organization, decreasing resistance, and the "buzz" on the success of the project.

♦ Ultimately, measure the behavior that drives your desired results.

HOW | **Agree on the metrics you will use and how you will collect and analyze data.**

How should we measure?

♦ Collect both quantitative and qualitative data. Use a variety of instruments, like:

- Surveys, focus groups, and interviews

- Observation, to record desired new behaviors

- Data that you're collecting anyway, like risk and issue tracking or system performance

- Key performance indicators and business metrics

- Milestones, money, work hours, and budgets.

♦ Collect baseline information to measure against, then measure more than once.

♦ Don't ignore your gut. If you and other project leaders feel something's going well, or going poorly, you're probably right.

WHEN | **Build in checkpoints for measurement. Budget time to measure and react to results.**

When should we measure?

- Identify checkpoints like:
  - Baseline
  - After a phase ends
  - After rollout or go-live
  - Three months out
  - Six months out.

- Build measurement time and responsibilities into the work plan.

- Plan to communicate upward and outward. Your goal is transparency and "no surprises."

- Resolve any issues and develop action plans, rolling them into the project plan.

Why should we measure?

♦ Celebrate success.

♦ Correct course, if needed.

♦ Explain business results and performance.

♦ Build a comprehensive story of the change, enhancing team member satisfaction and building institutional memory.

♦ Use as input for team member performance reviews.

♦ Justify future investments and initiatives.

♦ Compile "lessons learned" and improve future change projects.

The ugly truth about measurement

Everyone talks about it, but nobody does it. Why?

Because:

1. It's hard. You have to argue causality. How do you have a control group and interventions in a human performance system?

2. Someone might look bad. And get fired. Corporations don't like failure. Why take the risk?

3. It's expensive. If you do it right.

We recommend identifying one item from the business case—something that's high-impact and easy to do—and direct the change efforts at that item. Measure it. Start slowly and softly. Measurement is the holy grail, but right now, it's a glittering generality.

PACE Yourself!

The process and outputs of measurement have huge implications.

PUBLICATION

We can send findings to the organization or limit them to the team and management.

- Think about the impact on morale. Sometimes results are complex and multi-faceted. We might see significant benefits that aren't "sexy" near-term. If the data don't indicate a clear "win," will the organization feel their efforts were in vain?

- Show courtesy to those contributing data. Some information might have been shared with the assumption that it was confidential. Don't undermine future measurement efforts by betraying your friends. And some contributors expect a final report as a result of their input. A courtesy summary, even if mass distributed, is a thoughtful touch.

- Have the ability to act upon findings. Be prepared for, "Now what?" If results say there's a problem or an opportunity, consider pairing the results with next steps you can back up.

AGREEMENTS

Management must be aligned on what to do with the results prior to data gathering. Last minute reactions can confuse the organization.

- Is this a wedding or a funeral? Leaders must be clear on how to interpret, and portray results. When the time comes, they should know how they feel about the results and how they'd like people to feel. If messages aren't backed up by measurement, or people get different "vibes" from different leaders, it will deflate accomplishment and empowerment.

- Honor any implicit promises. Did leadership promise anything as a result of the initiative? To the organization, to customers, or to clients? What do the results say relative to those promises?

- Get it right inside the room. Leaders must decide, very specifically, which groups will take action based on the measurement results.

- Here we go again. How will new plans (to resolve what measurement has found) be received? As a new project? As another in a series of endless initiatives? Do you want to ask the same people to invest their energies again? Will announcing next steps will be empowering or exhausting?

CONSEQUENCES

Was unequivocal victory the only goal? Or will the organization celebrate and affirm a mixed result? How do you want your organization to feel as you approach your next initiative?

- If the team is punished for disappointing results, no one will risk "enlightenment" again.
- If the team is ignored following data collection, they will wonder why they bothered.
- If the intent is to create a "learning organization," everyone should celebrate the process of learning regardless of the result.

ENERGY

Objects at rest tend to stay at rest, objects in motion tend to stay in motion. Projects have a natural inertia. To take advantage of it, plan ahead. Frame at the outset what energy to direct at the outcome, and choose what actions to take or not take, so that the momentum doesn't stop. Response requires resources—time, people, will—the fabric of change over time. Energy enables that response.

P | **PUBLICATION**

A | **AGREEMENTS**

C | **CONSEQUENCES**

E | **ENERGY**

ABOUT THE AUTHORS

Trish Emerson has spent her career managing organizational change. Her passion is helping enhance the value of her clients' most important asset—their people. Trish so loves her chosen field that she launched her own firm: Emerson Human Capital Consulting, Inc. (EHC). Since 2001, EHC has provided organizations with creative solutions that bring tangible results.

Trish spends her free time maintaining her Victorian home in Alameda, California with her husband, while entertaining their son, an intrepid cat, and a constant stream of house guests.

Mary Stewart loves to talk about change. A former Big Five change management consultant, Mary now considers herself a writer and communicator. She has found her groove helping Emerson Human Capital reach out to clients and the consulting industry. She helps craft messages to clients, maintains EHC's branding and image, and supports the communication line of business.

Mary loves her work, but her true passions are raising her three children, finding and feeding two elusive cats, and spending time with her big, extended family in Oak Park, Illinois.